Veronica

the

Navy Sailor:

Making Waves of Change

Veronica V Scott

ISBN 979-8-9908746-0-2 (paperback)
ISBN 979-8-9908746-1-9 (hardcover)
ISBN 979-8-9908746-2-6 (eBook)

Printed in the United States of America

Thank You!

Thank you for purchasing this book! By doing so, you have contributed to and invested in the future generation of leaders. Half of the proceeds will go to the Association of Naval Services Officers (ANSO), an organization that I hold dear to my heart and that has helped me both personally and professionally. This is my way of giving back. What is ANSO? The Association of Naval Services Officers (ANSO) is dedicated to the professional development and advancement of Hispanic and Latino service members in the military. Our mission is to foster mentorship, leadership, and educational opportunities. Your support helps us provide JROTC Scholarships to young leaders, empowering them to achieve their dreams and serve our nation with pride.

Once upon a time in a small coastal town, in Oceanside, California there lived a little girl named Veronica.

Veronica had a heart as vast as the ocean and a dream as big as the sky. She wanted to make a difference in the world, just like the heroes she saw in her books and on TV.

Her dreams soared as high as the endless sky above her, fueled by a desire to make a difference in the world. Little did she know her journey would lead her to the most extraordinary adventure of all.

Sailor
and
The Navy

Veronica's eyes sparkled with wonder as she delved into tales of courageous Sailors who sailed the seas and made a difference in the world. Each page turned filled her with a sense of pride and excitement. She imagined herself as one of those brave Sailors, protecting the oceans and helping people in need. In that moment, Veronica knew that one day she too could accomplish great things and become a Sailor.

Crayon
Paper
Marker
8

Veronica loved spending time in her room, especially when she sat at her desk by the window with a view of the ocean. With her pencils and papers spread out, she spent hours drawing pictures of amazing ships and brave Sailors in her notebook. Each stroke of her pencil filled her with excitement, imagining herself as part of their adventures.

But Veronica didn't just dream of adventures; she also thought about how she could make a difference in the world. So, beside her drawings, she made a list of all the things she wanted to do to help others and make the world a better place. And as she looked out at the vast sea beyond her window, she knew that one day, joining the Navy could be her way of turning those dreams into reality.

One sunny afternoon, Veronica gathered her courage and sat down with her parents in the cozy living room. With excitement bubbling inside her, she shared her big dream of becoming a Navy Sailor. With her hands waving in enthusiasm, Veronica explained how she wanted to protect the sea and make a positive difference in the world.

Her parents listened intently, their eyes shining with pride and love. They encouraged Veronica to follow her heart and pursue her dreams, knowing that with determination and passion, she could achieve anything she set her mind to. And as Veronica spoke, she felt even more certain that joining the Navy was the path she wanted to take to turn her dreams into reality.

Veronica's heart swelled with happiness as her parents knelt down beside her, wrapping her in their warm embrace. With gentle smiles on their faces, they spoke words of encouragement that filled Veronica with confidence and hope.

"We believe in you, Veronica," her parents said softly. "If you want to become a Navy Sailor and make the world a better place, we'll be right here beside you, supporting you every step of the way."

Feeling the love and support of her family, Veronica's determination to pursue her dream of joining the Navy grew even stronger. With her parents by her side, she knew that she could overcome any challenge and achieve greatness.

JOIN THE
U.S. NAVY
TODAY!
GARCIA

With a brave heart and determination guiding her, Veronica walked into the Navy recruitment office. She sat down at a desk across from a friendly Navy Recruiter, who greeted her with a warm smile.

As Veronica shared her dreams of becoming a Navy Sailor, the Recruiter listened attentively. With excitement shining in their eyes, they told Veronica all about the amazing adventures and opportunities that awaited her in the Navy.

Veronica's heart raced with excitement as she listened, imagining herself sailing across the seas and making a difference in the world. With each word from the Recruiter, her dreams of joining the Navy grew even stronger.

SCOTT

After months of dedication and hard work, Veronica's dream finally came true. With a sense of pride swelling in her chest, she stood tall in her Navy Sailor uniform, ready to embark on her journey. With each button she fastened, she felt a sense of purpose wash over her.

As Veronica looked at herself in the mirror, she couldn't help but feel like a real-life hero. With her name proudly displayed on her uniform, as "Petty Officer Scott", she knew she was part of something bigger than herself. She was ready to set sail, protect the seas, and help those in need.

SCOTT
U.S NAVY
WHITE
U.S NAVY
NOBLE
U.S NAVY

Every day aboard the USS Navy ship was an adventure for Veronica. With her name proudly displayed on her uniform, she worked alongside her fellow Sailors, like Chief White and Master Chief Noble, to keep the seas safe for everyone.

From learning to navigate the vast oceans to assisting her shipmates in various tasks, Veronica faced exciting challenges that helped her grow stronger and more capable. With each passing day, she realized the importance of teamwork and dedication in protecting the seas and ensuring the safety of all who sailed upon them.

NAVY
NAVY

Veronica and her Shipmates had big hearts for the environment. They knew that keeping the beaches clean was important for protecting sea creatures and preserving nature's beauty.

So, during their free time, Veronica and her friends grabbed their trash bags and headed to the beach. With determination in their hearts, they worked together to pick up litter and make a difference. Whether it was plastic bottles or stray wrappers, they made sure to leave the beach better than they found it.

Veronica felt proud knowing that she was not only serving her country but also taking care of the world around her. And as they worked side by side, she realized that making a difference didn't always mean big actions—it could start with something as simple as cleaning up a beach.

As the wind howled and the rain poured down, Veronica and her Shipmates received a distress call. Without hesitation, they sprang into action, knowing that people were counting on them for help.

Braving the stormy seas, they rushed to aid those stranded at sea. With their teamwork and bravery, they faced the raging elements head—on, determined to make a difference.

Despite the challenging conditions, Veronica and her friends never gave up. Their unwavering courage and quick thinking saved lives that night, proving that even in the darkest of storms, heroes emerge to shine a light of hope.

SCOTT

Veronica's heart swelled with pride as she stood before her fellow Sailors, receiving the prestigious Medal. With a beaming smile, she accepted the medal, knowing it was a symbol of her dedication and courage in making the world a better place.

The medal glistened in the light, representing all the good she had done to protect the seas and help those in need. Veronica felt honored to receive such recognition for her service, and it only fueled her determination to continue making a difference, one act of kindness at a time.

SCOTT

Veronica's heart swelled with joy as she stood beside her parents, feeling proud of all she had achieved. Her dream of becoming a United States Navy Sailor had finally come true, and she knew she had made a real difference in the world, just like she had always hoped.

As she looked into her parents' eyes, she saw nothing but love and pride reflected back at her. With their unwavering support and encouragement, Veronica had overcome challenges and reached for the stars. Now, as a Sailor, she was ready to continue her journey of service and make even more waves of change in the world.

SCOTT

As Veronica stood by the beach once again, she realized that anyone, no matter how small, could make waves of change in the world. All it took was a big dream and the courage to chase it.

SCOTT

Veronica loved sharing stories of her adventures in the Navy with her fellow fifth graders. Dressed in her crisp U.S. Navy Dress Blue uniform, she stood tall in front of the classroom, her eyes sparkling with excitement.

"Did you know that in the Navy, you can travel to far-off places and learn new things every day?" Veronica exclaimed, her voice filled with enthusiasm. "You can be a part of something bigger than yourself and make a real difference in the world!"

The children leaned in, captivated by Veronica's tales of bravery and service. They imagined themselves sailing across the ocean, exploring distant lands, and working together as a team to overcome any challenge.

Inspired by Veronica's words, the students felt a sense of pride and possibility. They realized that they, too, could follow their dreams and pursue exciting opportunities in the Navy or any other path they chose.

And so, Veronica continued to inspire all students, showing them that with courage, determination, and a little bit of imagination, they could achieve anything they set their minds to. With each story she shared, she sparked a sense of adventure and ambition in the hearts of the fifth graders, encouraging them to dream big and reach for the stars.

The End

CAR
SCOTT
FRA

As Veronica's story comes to a close, remember that each one of you holds the power to chase your dreams and make a difference. Just like Veronica, you can overcome challenges, follow your heart, and achieve greatness.

Whether it's protecting the seas, serving your community, or pursuing your passions, know that the world is full of endless possibilities waiting for you to explore. So, dream big, work hard, and never give up on making your mark on the world.

Remember, you are capable of greatness. Believe in yourself, and one day, you might find yourself standing tall like Veronica, ready to embark on your own extraordinary journey.

Go forth with courage and kindness, for you are the future leaders who will shape our world for the better. Adventure awaits—are you ready to set sail?

Dream big, little Sailors, and never forget: the world is yours to explore and change for the better.

www.ingramcontent.com/pod-product-compliance
Lightning Source LLC
Chambersburg PA
CBHW041631110726
48005CB00002B/562